Great Explo

written by David Neufeld   *illustrated by Nora Koerber*

SCHOLASTIC INC.
New York   Toronto   London   Auckland   Sydney
Mexico City   New Delhi   Hong Kong   Buenos Aires

Developed by Kirchoff/Wohlberg, Inc., in cooperation with Scholastic Inc.

Copyright © 2002 by Scholastic Inc.
All rights reserved.   Published by Scholastic Inc.   Printed in the U.S.A.
ISBN 0-439-35178-2
SCHOLASTIC and associated logos and designs are trademarks
and/or registered trademarks of Scholastic Inc.
18 19 20 21   40   16 15 14 13

Have you ever looked at the horizon and wondered what was out there? People have been curious about the unknown for centuries. People who explore the unknown are sometimes called navigators. Navigators know where they are, know where they are going, and know how to get back from there. For centuries, navigators were most interested in sailing the seas.

The ancient Polynesians might sail a thousand miles and find an island no bigger than an airport. We have learned that their instruments could sense ripples from waves breaking on an island 200 miles away. They made charts from woven reeds and shells. They looked at the stars to figure out where they were. They used the sun as well.

The Vikings

In 982 A.D., the Vikings set out across the Atlantic Ocean. The word "Viking" means "pirate." Eric the Red, one of the first Viking navigators, was not the kind of person you'd want for a neighbor. He was so warlike that he was banished from Norway. He sailed away from home in search of what all pirates seek: riches.

Eric knew of a distant land called Thule. It had been discovered by a Greek explorer named Pytheas a thousand years earlier. Over the years, seafaring people had brought many valuable walrus tusks and polar bear pelts from Thule back to Norway.

Sailing across the North Atlantic was dangerous business for Eric. He followed the setting sun toward Thule. He knew a treasure of walruses, seals, falcons, and bears awaited him. The Vikings called this country Iceland.

Viking ships sailed with the winds. Their square sails carried them along. The only way home was to find a wind blowing the opposite way.

This often meant waiting until the seasons changed. Sailors lived by the wind. Early compasses were called wind roses. They were many-pointed stars that gave names to all the winds.

Vikings also sailed by the stars, particularly the North Star. The North Star always told sailors which direction north was.

They would also use a notched stick to help them stay on course. First they would hold the stick in the air. Then they would measure the number of notches they saw between the horizon and the North Star. Counting notches would help the sailors figure out their location on the globe.

After sailing for many days, the Vikings finally landed at Iceland. This country was a beautiful island with green pastures below snow-capped mountains. It wasn't long before the Vikings stayed there for the winter.

Eric was always a warlike fellow, though. The more peaceable settlers on Iceland eventually convinced him to leave. He built a base on Greenland, a place not at all green and very harsh. His son, Leif Ericsson, would sail far from that place, even reaching what we now call North America.

The descendants of Eric the Red's Vikings still live on Iceland and Greenland. They have turned to farming and fishing.

Prince Henry the Navigator

Prince Henry of Portugal had a comfortable life. However, he went to great lengths to find out more about the unknown.

In the 1420s Henry gathered every known piece of nautical information. He asked captains and mapmakers from all over the Mediterranean coast to bring him information about uncharted waters.

One place Henry was interested in was the southern portion of Africa. In Henry's day, sailors believed a dangerous, shallow ocean there prevented anyone from sailing around the southern tip of Africa to India. Some thought it was the end of the earth.

Henry sent ships and captains to test those stories. Finally, one brave captain made it past the shallows. Imagine his surprise when the whole Southern Ocean opened up!

Prince Henry built a tower on a cliff above the Atlantic. It became a research station. Navigators from many different countries were all welcome. Henry demanded accuracy.

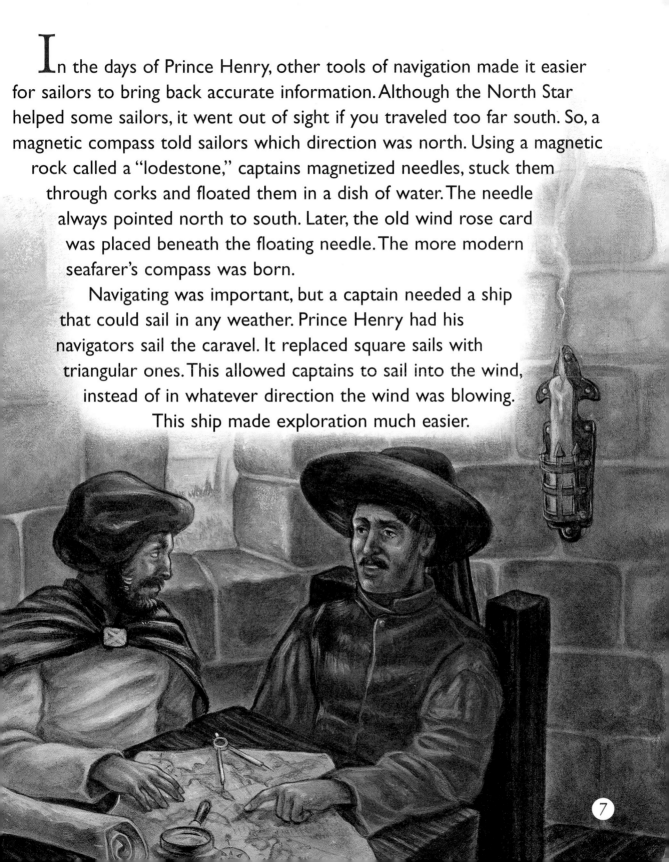

In the days of Prince Henry, other tools of navigation made it easier for sailors to bring back accurate information. Although the North Star helped some sailors, it went out of sight if you traveled too far south. So, a magnetic compass told sailors which direction was north. Using a magnetic rock called a "lodestone," captains magnetized needles, stuck them through corks and floated them in a dish of water. The needle always pointed north to south. Later, the old wind rose card was placed beneath the floating needle. The more modern seafarer's compass was born.

Navigating was important, but a captain needed a ship that could sail in any weather. Prince Henry had his navigators sail the caravel. It replaced square sails with triangular ones. This allowed captains to sail into the wind, instead of in whatever direction the wind was blowing. This ship made exploration much easier.

Christopher Columbus

In the 1480s, Christopher Columbus was eager to explore the unknown. At that time, there was a lot of it. Many charts showed huge areas of unmapped land and water.

Columbus wanted to find an easy trade route between Spain and the Indies. Explorers at that time thought the Indies were composed of China, Japan, India, and numerous small islands. Columbus said he would get there by sailing west. Most European explorers thought the only way to sail there was by sailing east, around the southern tip of Africa— which was thought to be a long and difficult voyage. Few of them tried it.

According to Columbus's calculations, the trip to Japan would be around 3,000 miles. He thought it would be much easier than sailing around Africa. Of course, the world was much bigger than Columbus thought it was. As you will see, he made some honest mistakes. His mistakes, though, led to some of the earliest explorations of the Americas.

Columbus made four voyages. On each voyage, he made different discoveries.

On the first voyage, he claimed San Salvador, an island of the Bahamas, for Spain. Because he thought he had reached the Indies, he called the people he met there "Indians." Later during that same voyage, he landed on Cuba. At the time, he thought he was in China.

On the second voyage, Columbus found Jamaica. He also founded Isabela, on the island of Hispaniola, the first European settlement in the Americas.

Columbus explored South America and Central America during his last two voyages. He brought his thirteen-year-old son on his fourth voyage. His son wrote an accurate description of the trip that became an important source for future scholars.

To keep himself on course when he was out of sight of land, Columbus used a navigation method called "dead reckoning."

To dead reckon, sailors would mark on a chart a place that they knew, such as an island. Once the island was out of sight, they tied a piece of wood to a line. They threw the wood overboard at the front of the ship. They recorded the time it took the wood to float to the back of the ship. By dividing the length of the ship by the time recorded, they could calculate speed.

Dead reckoning was not a very accurate method of determining speed. However, it kept Columbus and his sailors going in the direction they wanted to travel.

Vasco Da Gama

Vasco da Gama promised his Portuguese king that he would establish an ocean route to India. Before his journey, all trade goods from the East came over land to Europe. This was a long and expensive way to go. The cargo that a caravan could carry was limited in weight and size.

A 200-ton ship could carry almost anything. Vasco da Gama set out with four ships. He traveled to India by sailing around the coast of Africa. Aboard his ship were many stone pillars. He set these pillars along the African coast as markers.

It took da Gama ten months to reach India. He met with royal leaders and traded for spices and gems.

Vasco da Gama left Portugal with 170 men, but only 55 lived to see home. Many of them got scurvy. Scurvy was a disease caused by a lack of vitamin C. Months aboard a ship with only dried meat and biscuits made the sailors sick.

After da Gama returned, he had maps drawn of the Indian Ocean and the Atlantic coast. These maps were available to Portuguese sailors only. They were so secret that anyone caught sharing Portuguese charts would be put to death.

Magellan

Ferdinand Magellan was both a fine navigator and a wise leader.

He led an expedition to claim the Spice Islands, near what is now Australia, for Spain.

On September 20, 1519, he set out with five ships. With him he carried about 250 men, 35 magnetized needles, and one writer who would record the entire journey.

From the Canary Islands off the northern coast of Africa, he sailed west by his compass for Brazil. Carefully, he sailed down the coast of South America. He charted every inlet. He stopped twice: once to take on fresh food and water, and again when there was a mutiny.

Magellan sent a ship ahead into the straits to scout the route. They were anything but straight. Time after time, a dead end would appear. Craggy islands dotted the channel. The narrows at the western end were at places only two miles wide. Strong winds called "williwaws" squeezed between cliffs. A sudden blast from one could flip a ship over.

Magellan was looking for a channel through the continent. What he found is now known as the Strait of Magellan. To every sailor in the world, even today, these are the most respected and feared waters on the planet. They lie between the southern tip of South America and a small island off the coast.

Magellan got three of the five ships through. One of the other ships was wrecked in a storm, while the last one deserted the expedition and returned to Spain. Ahead of him lay a vast, peaceful ocean. He named it the Pacific Ocean. Magellan headed north and then westward into the ocean. His instinct for following winds was amazing. The course he plotted from the Strait of Magellan across the unknown Pacific is the same course recommended for sailors today!

On September 8, 1522, three years after Magellan's departure, eighteen men arrived in Seville, Spain. Of the original 250 men, these were the only survivors. Magellan was not among them.

Many had starved because they had been given only one-third of the supplies they had paid for on their stop in South America. By the time they discovered that fact, they were nearly out of food and nowhere near help.

Magellan himself had survived mutiny, hunger, and the almost unimaginable size of the Pacific Ocean. But he died during an attack by locals on the Phillipine island of Mactan, where his men had landed temporarily.

In a thousand years, navigators have gone from using a notched stick, the sun, and the stars to the modern Global Positioning System (GPS). Just as the ancient navigators used stars and planets as guides, the GPS system receives signals from satellites in outer space.

As we continue to navigate uncharted regions of Earth and space, the principle remains the same. We choose known objects as landmarks. The more objects we use, the better. If you know where they are on your map or chart, you will know where you are. As we learn to navigate more and more efficiently, the world—and what lies beyond it—will be less and less mysterious.